The Complete Guide

To

REPUBLICAN ETHICS

The Complete Guide

To

REPUBLICAN ETHICS

R.G. Fredericks

JezzieLu Press
Los Angeles, CA

Published in the United States of America
by JezzieLu Press

ISBN: 978-0-9983254-0-8   paperback

*Dedicated to the day that Republicans
start showing any signs of ethics.*

Any sign.

Any.

We may have a long wait.

This page is intentionally blank

.... and so is this one

.... and this one

.... and this one

.... and this one

.... and this one

.... and this one

.... and this one

.... and this one

.... and this one

.... and this one

.... and this one

.... and this one

.... and this one

.... and this one

.... and this one

.... and this one

.... and this one

.... and this one

.... and this one

.... and this one

.... and this one

.... and this one

.... and this one

.... and this one

.... and this one

.... and this one

.... and this one

.... and this one

.... and this one

.... and this one

.... and this one

.... and this one

.... and this one

.... and this one

.... and this one

.... and this one

.... and this one

.... and this one

.... and this one

.... and this one

.... and this one

.... and this one

.... and this one

.... and this one

.... and this one

.... and this one

.... and this one

.... and this one

.... and this one

.... and this one

.... and this one

.... and this one

.... and this one

.... and this one

.... and this one

.... and this one

.... and this one

.... and this one

.... and this one

.... and this one

.... and this one

.... and this one

.... and this one

.... and this one

.... and this one

.... and this one

.... and this one

.... and this one

.... and this one

.... and this one

.... and this one

.... and this one

.... and this one

.... and this one

.... and this one

.... and this one

.... and this one

.... and this one

.... and this one

.... and this one

.... and this one

.... and this one

.... and this one

.... and this one

.... and this one

.... and this one

.... and this one

.... and this one

.... and this one

.... and this one

.... and this one

.... and this one

.... and this one

.... and this one

.... and this one

.... and this one

.... and this one

.... and this one

.... and this one

.... and this one

.... and this one

.... and this one

.... and this one

.... and this one

.... and this one

.... and this one

.... and this one

.... and this one

.... and this one

.... and this one

.... and this one

.... and this one

.... and this one

.... and this one

.... and this one

.... and this one

.... and this one

.... and this one

.... and this one

.... and this one

.... and this one

.... and finally, this one too.

The Complete Guide

To

REPUBLICAN
ETHICS

For more, please launch another
worthless, expensive, politically-inspired, democracy-damaging
investigation on over to

www.RepublicanEthics.com

Made in the USA
Las Vegas, NV
05 December 2021